The Chaos is Beautiful

OTHER BOOKS BY ROBERT M. DRAKE

Spaceship (2012)

Science (2013)

Beautiful Chaos (2014)

Black Butterfly (2015)

A Brilliant Madness (2015)

Beautiful and Damned (2016)

Broken Flowers (2016)

Seed Of Chaos (2017)

Gravity: A Novel (2017)

Moon Theory (2017)

Young & Rebellious (2018)

Chasing The Gloom (2018)

Samuel White & The Frog King (2018)

For Excerpts and Updates please follow:

Instagram.com/rmdrk
Facebook.com/rmdrk
Twitter.com/rmdrk

ISBN: 978-0-9986293-8-4

Book Cover: Robert M. Drake
Cover Image licensed by Shutter Stock Inc.

For My Sisters

CONTENTS

BEAUTIFUL CHAOS 2

ROBERT M. DRAKE

HOW MUCH I DO NOT CARE

I know you
came back to tell me
how much you
still care.

But you have to understand
how that is hard for me
to believe.

You took my soul.

You broke it down,
devoured it.

Then you abandon it,
left it out
in the sun to die.

To slowly fade away.

Too careless.
Too reckless.
Too weak to hold.

And then
there's my heart

you left so many knives

you would wonder
how in the hell
I was still alive.

How in the hell it
was still alive.

I wish someone
had told me
about this.

About the process.

About…
the getting over
and letting go.

The breaking.
The healing.
The forgetting.

I wish someone
had warned me
about you.

Warned me
about your wit
and charm.

Warned me
about this funky

little thing
called depression
and anxiety.

I wish someone was there
for me during that time.

Hell…

and now you're here.

A few months later
telling me
how different things could be,

that is,
if I give it another shot.

Gave you another chance.

I laugh.

Not because it is funny
but because
I have no idea

what to think
other than how selfish
you are.

I laugh…

and I do because
it's funny to me

how you think
I'm the same.

It's funny to me
how you think
you can manipulate
the situation

and make yourself believe
that what you did
was okay.

That the past is the past.

Shit that's funny, too funny.

You want another chance?
For me to give you my trust?
Again?

To give you
whatever it is
I have left?

Goddamn,
I am speechless
and you should win

an Oscar for the bullshit
performance you just gave.

I'm sorry.
At least
I'm honest
but in all honesty,

I have run out of *fucks*
to give.

So breathe.
Inhale, and take this in
slowly…

the mother fucking world
doesn't revolve around you.

It never will
and it never has.

The sun is still here.
The clouds.
The dirt.
The Earth.

And so am I.

Hallelujah. Hallelujah. Hallelujah.

And yes,

love is always the answer
but not tonight.

Tonight
it is all about me
and tonight

I could care less
of your feelings...

mother fucker.

YOU REALLY DON'T

You don't have to be
with someone
if you're alone.

You don't need to feel
as if
you need to find
someone new

when someone has
abandoned you.

People leave,
and we know this
already
but that doesn't mean

once someone is out
the door
that you must open it
to let
a new lover in.

That's another
goddamn tragedy
waiting to happen.

So give yourself

some time to breathe
a little,

to live
a little on your own.

Give yourself some space,
a tiny bit of it.
It will do you some good.

Give yourself time,
all the seconds
and all the hours
of the day.

Give yourself a chance,
the patience you need
to heal, to move on...

your way,
and at your own pace.

Is it that hard to do?

To just do it.
Day in and day out.
To live by it.

You don't need someone
to be happy,
to feel complete.

You don't need to rely
on another human being
to find what fuels you.

You don't.
Really, you don't.

And yes,
people are addicting.
There's no lie in that.

But what matters most
is *you...*

and I will say this...
time and time again.

People aren't meant
to complete you.

They aren't meant
to define you.

They aren't meant
to fix you, to heal you

or to bring you back
from some terrible doom.

They are meant to guide you.
To be there for you.

To witness your flaws
and appreciate you
for who you are…

regardless

of what happens
in the end.

People,
like years,
they come and they go

but what you have
within matters most.

And I hope
you take the time

you need
to realize this

because

you don't need someone
to fill the void...

that is,
after all,

something only

you can do…

for yourself.

FEEL THEM

Some wounds
never heal.

You just learn
how to live with them.

You go to a place
where you barely

feel them at all.

Where you barely
recognize yourself

and die a little slower
each night

because you miss
the one you love.

WILL CHANGE

You keep telling yourself
that maybe one day

the person you love
will change.

Maybe one day
they'll finally see

what you see,
feel what you feel

and regret all the wrong
they've done to you.

You keep telling yourself
it'll be okay—that giving them time

will make them grow
and appreciate you

for who you are.

You keep telling yourself
that maybe one day

everything will change
for the best,

and that the both of you
will finally come to terms

and *be happy.*

You keep telling yourself
this and that

but this is where it hurts.

Where it stings a little harder
because you've been telling yourself

this for years
and deep down inside

you know
that at some point

you're going to have to come
to the realization

that some people
aren't meant to be yours.

No matter how much
history you have.

No matter how hard you try,
and how many nights you've shared
beneath the moon.

Because at some point…
you're going to find yourself
wanting more, wanting better.

That's human nature
and you can only tolerate so much

until you finally
snap out of it.

And it could happen at anytime.

A week from now,
a month

or even a year later.

And when that day comes,
you will tell yourself

how important your past was.

You will tell yourself
how big of a role

the people who've hurt you had.

And maybe you'll even thank them.

Maybe you'll even wonder
how different your life

could have been without them.

And you will accept everything,
both bad and good,

and forgive them
and forgive yourself as well.

You will move on.
You will know what you deserve.

And you will finally
open those beautiful eyes of yours
and see for the very first time.

Change will be brewing
over the horizon
 and everyone who has ever hurt you

will appear before you,
and you will quietly whisper:

*"I should have never fought so hard
for those who never loved me*

*and I should have given myself
the time I needed to heal.*

Nonetheless,

I want to thank you

for hurting me the way you did.
I'm a better person now

and I could have not done it
without you."

BEFORE YOUR EYES

Growth is more
than just a word

and the passage of time.

It is the outcome
of a broken heart.

The next day
after a long night
full of tears.

And the desire to rise
after watching everything

you've worked
for shatter

right before your eyes.

YOU WANT BUT YOU CAN'T

You want to take them back
but you know nothing has changed.

And nothing ever will
if you do.

That's how love goes.
That's how life is.

Sometimes
you get too damn comfortable
with people

and jobs and places
and everything in general.

You get so used to seeing
the same things over and over.

Day in and day out.

Then you begin to ignore,
and forget their value.

Please,
with every fiber in your being,

do not become

this kind of person.

Do not overlook
the beauty everything has
to offer.

Do not become someone
who doesn't have the courage

to even consider
this type of thinking.

It's the way of life.

A rare paradigm
that only the broken accept.

Try new things.

Go out and take the risk.

On people,
places and experience.

It is crucial
to not live this boring life.

This nine-to-five lifestyle
we are all born to believe in.
Life is so much better
than that.

I vouch to this
and drink to this.

Believe me.
There's so much more.

All you have to do
is believe

and soon enough

everything you've
ever dreamed of

will be yours.

WHY CHANGE

You can't change people.

Assholes
are going to be
assholes.

Rebels
are going to be
rebels.

And loners
are going to be
loners, man.

But you can change
your perception of them.

And how all of them
don't want to be alone.

All of them need someone
or something

to love.

No matter what they say
or don't say.

TEARING YOU UP

I could tell something is
tearing you up inside.

Something terrible.

Something from your past
 is haunting you

day in and day out.

I could see it in your sad eyes.
In your sad smile.

Something is hurting you
and it's eating you alive
without remorse.

Let it be known,
that always in me,
you have a friend.

That always in me,
you have someone to talk to—

someone to listen
to what's aching your heart.

Let it be known,

that whatever it is
you're going through…
it is something

you no longer
have to go through alone.

Let it be known,
my friend,

that I am here with you

and I always have been,
and I will never leave your side

no matter how tragic
life gets.

A MESSAGE ON FACEBOOK

I get a dm.

One girl tells me
I am god.

That I always know
what she feels.

That my words
always come to her
at the right moment.

Soon after
I get another dm.

Another girl tells me
that my work is trash

and that's all she writes
in the message.

I don't know what it is.

What I do.
Why I write.

Why I even read
their messages.

People are funny,
confused little creatures.

They either *love*
or hate

what they *don't understand.*

PEACE IN

You've got to work on yourself
day by day.

You've got to remember
that your entire life

is a work in progress.

That you're going to have
bad days but also good ones

to balance everything out.

You've got to know
that sometimes you're going to get
your heart broken.

While other times,
you're the one

who's going to be breaking
someone else's.

You've got to accept
that nothing ever goes as planned

and that *nothing* is perfect.
You've got to realize

that what you feel
is never wrong

and you must always trust
your intuition

but also accept
the consequence of things.

You've got to know
that it's never too late

to be where you want to be.

To become
who you want
to become.

To feel
what you want
to feel

and to love
the way you want
to be loved:

Both freely
and without discrimination.

You've got to believe in this,
live by this

and listen to your voice
when you have to.

In all shapes and forms.

You've got to empower
every human you love

and empower yourself
to be good
to those you don't love.

To be good, you know?

And let everything that brings
the light closer to you,

and everything
that brings you peace…

in.

STILL HERE

You're still here,
in this goddamn forsaken city.

And you're still walking,
breathing and living,

no matter how much
it hurts inside.

You're still you.

You're still fighting,
trying to maintain—

waking up each day
and telling yourself

it's okay,
because it is.

You're still recovering.

You're still realizing your worth—
no matter how many times
you've been let down.

You're still here, goddammit!

Young and beautiful.

Full of pain
and full of laughter.

Cold and broken
but never alone.

The struggle is real.

You are real.
What you feel is real.

And you must realize your strength
and how you are capable of moving on.

You must realize the beauty
of finding yourself

and your natural ability to heal.

You must realize
how special you are,

and how you value yourself…
is the most important thing

in the world.

Always.

A CALL FROM HEX

The phone rang.

I woke up to get it
without knowing
what time is was.

"Goddamn, fucking neighbors
have just woken me up."

It was my cousin, Hex.

He's been complaining
about his new neighbors
for the last two weeks.

"Can you fucking believe this?"

I stayed quiet
trying to focus my eyes.

"They've been waking me up
in the middle of the night…
with all their *fucking* noise."

I turned toward the clock
with the phone on my hands.

It said 4:21 a.m.

"Don't they fucking
know what time it is?

It's too late for this
type of shit.

Waking me up in the
middle of the night!"

He ranted, and never
did the exhaustion
find him.

I guess some people
don't notice what they do
until it's done to them.

While other people
will keep doing it

no matter who
tells them what.

LIVE BY THIS, DIE BY THIS

As long as I am with you
I have nothing

to worry about.

Therefore,
the world could burn

and the birds can fall
from the sky.

I got you,
right now,

here in my arms
and we're surviving
through the destruction.

We are holding on
to what really matters,

to each other.

To our fears and desires.

I love that
because I need
that type of flame.

Flawed and in love.

We are alive
and there's nothing better

to live by
than that.

WYNWOOD AGAIN

Lost in a sunset.

In the lovely city
of Wynwood

I stand in the middle
of Wood Tavern
with a half empty drink
in my hand.

The tunes flow…
they drip like honey
falling from the speakers.

The lights twinkle
fading in and out of the darkness.

I mind my business.

My comrades…

misunderstood
angry
and beaten.

They are worn
from the nine-to-five.

The sounds of music
are continuous…

they flow like the liquor
within the blood.

A brunette
friend of a friend
has found us in the crowd.

She walks over
swiftly,
flawlessly,
like a goddess
parting the sea.

She does small talk
with a mutual comrade of ours.

I pay no attention.

Time passes by
and I caught her attention…

she asked for my name

what I do
and why I look so mad.

I am quiet.

Alone, here,
although my comrades
are with me

but nonetheless, alone.

She asks me
why I am so serious…

if something was bothering me
and what was on my mind.

I tip the bartender
ask for another drink
and offered her one, too.

She asks for wine,
red wine.

I hate red wine.

I turn around
pass her drink and say.

"It's not that I'm mad.

The question is,
how could you not be,
with everything that's going on.

Anger is all I could feel.

The killings printed on paper.

The blood captured on video…
the mockery of life and death.

We entertain ourselves
with another man's tragic demise.

And then
we share it on social media
to pretend we care.

To say we need a change.

And we do,
but none of us want to take
that leap.

None of us want to risk
what we barely have.

Everyone is afraid,
waiting for someone

to do something about it,
anyone,
as long as it's not them.

And that's the problem here,"

I say as her face drops.

Of course,
that's the reaction I expected.

Of course,
I never planned to see her again.

She slowly stepped out of my frame
and I let her do so without hesitation.

Because I was too busy
thinking of this verse

when I got home

and she was too busy
pretending

she was listening
to what I said.

I WANT TO...

I want you to feel—
to remember what it was like

when you first laid eyes on
something you loved.

I want you to breathe,
to inhale.

To run your fingers
through the air

and collect the memories
as they pass you by.

I want you to remember

the way we spoke.

The way we looked
into our eyes
as the scent filled

the empty
space in the room.

I want you to feel it.
To remember it.

To be
attracted to it.

I want the company
of me,

to remind you

how to live,
how to laugh,

and above all,
how to love.

LEFT BEHIND

I look far away
and remember what
you left behind.

I remember the ocean breeze.

The waves
and the falling
of rain.

With deep breaths
and steady thoughts.

The heart skips
and never desires
to slip away.

You hold me
and with one slow inhale
I am taken back—

I am reminded of everyone
I have ever loved,

of everything
I have ever wanted.

Your fragrance has me.

It pulls me in and out
of my past, my future.

And the moment
you're gone
my night is never the same.

In all rawness
and love…

what I'm trying to say is,

even after we part
your scent pushes me
toward the light…

lost,
drunk in love,

and lingering
in a place

where only
the flowers
can grow.

FLOWERS AGAIN

This is about the flowers
and the way
the wind blows the petals
as they fall.

This is about the rain
and the sound it makes
as it hits the window.

This is about
the last car ride home

and the way it makes you
reminisce of all the
places you miss.

This is about laughter
and the way it triggers feelings

you once had
as a child.

This is about people
and the way

their hands hold on to one another
without knowing
when to let go.

This is about love…

the way two people
find one another

and the way they
lose themselves in

a garden full of roses.

This is about you.

About your life.

About the way you look,
the way you feel

and

the way your scent fills
the room.

YOU DESERVE THIS

The way you need
to be loved

and the way you want
are two very different things.

One you can learn
to live without

while the other
will take a lifetime
to accept.

You have to listen to yourself,
to what you need,
feel,

to be willing
to lose yourself

the kind of love
you deserve.

DO YOU SOME GOOD

I hope you find someone
who's real with you.

Someone who's capable
of telling you
when you're wrong,

when you're about
to make a mistake.

I hope you find someone
who's not afraid to love.

Someone who's not afraid
to get hurt.

I hope you find more
than just a lover.

I hope you find a friend,
and I hope they love you,
really love you

and I hope they love
themselves as well.

I hope you find someone
who cares—

not just someone
who cares about you

but also someone
who cares about others.

Someone who cares
about making a difference,

about leaving
some kind of mark
on the world:

to heal it,
change it for the best.

In the most genuine way,
I hope someone like this
finds you,

whether you're searching for them
or not.

Because there are so many reasons
for you to be happy.

So many chances
to let go of everything
that brings you down.

I hope you let

"being in love"

with the right person
be a small part

of something

that's meant
to do you
some good.

THE...

The birds fly.
The leaves fall.

The seasons change.
The wind causes friction
on my skin.

The sun rotates.

It hides.
It appears.

It shines
no matter what.

The oceans feel ease.
The waves flow
and most of the time,

I am here,

thinking

about you.

CHASE THE STARS IN PEOPLE

Kid,
I gave you
what you asked for.

What you wanted.

I gave you my heart
and you had it.

Sadly
you let it slip away.

Some people chase something
their entire lives

and when they finally find it,
they lose it.

They regret it

and realize
what they've lost

as soon as it's
gone.

AFTER TOMORROW

After tomorrow,
a new year starts.

After tomorrow,
a new opportunity arises.

After tomorrow,
a new version of you
is born.

Take what you've learned
this year and heal from it.

Grow from it.

And understand
how beautiful it is
to reach this point—

to stand and inhale
the life you've been granted.

Let this new year
be *your* year.

Let it be the second chance
you've been wanting to take.
Let it be

the answers
you've been looking for.

Let this New Year
consume you.

Let it guide you.

And let it give you
the hope you need

to move forward.

After tomorrow,
it begins,

and you must know
how only the best

is yet to come.

ENTIRE LIFE

You spend your whole life
worrying about being alone

that you've let
so many good people
pass you by.

The same way you've spent
so much time
thinking of those who don't care

rather than the ones
who do.

And this is what your life
has turned into.

Chasing people
who don't understand you

while overlooking

the ones who relate
to you the most.

You've let so much
time slip,

you've let too many
people slip,

and now you're slipping yourself...

by chasing people
who've caused you the most harm.

When does it end?

When do you finally realize
who you are?

Who you deserve?
Does it ever stop?

The pain.
The brokenness.

The emptiness
and the longing of being
understood—of being

held by the right hands.

I get you.

You feel like the ocean—
the rain

but that doesn't mean

you've got to drown on your own.

With water comes life.
And with pain comes love.

So hang in there,
my sweet friend...

life isn't meant
to destroy you.

People aren't meant
to hurt you...

and all the things you feel
aren't meant to bring you closer

to your doom.

Because everything around you
is a lesson waiting to be learned,

and how you let them
affect you

is completely up to you.

So cry now and laugh later...
it's okay...

because something better

is on the way.

Just stay humble,
learn from your mistakes

and keep your heart open
for when the right

opportunities come.

ALMOST DELETED

A girl sends me
a message in Instagram.

She says,

"Where do you get
your inspiration?"

I reply.

"Life, my dear, life."

My laughter.
My sweat.
My tears.

My pain.
My love.
My loss.

My gain.
My experience,
and my writing.

Will always

be based on
life.

BEAUTIFUL HUMAN

Beautiful human beings
come and go.

So there is no reason
to believe they were
the one.

You're going to think that
about everyone
you fall in love with.

You're going to believe
that's "the one" each time.

And then,
this is how it usually happens.

Like five years pass
and suddenly,

you open your eyes
for the first time.

You find yourself laughing
a little harder.

Holding hands
a little tighter

and growing with one person
for the past few years.

And for reasons unknown,
it always feels
as if

time has flown by
far too quickly.

You spend several years
with someone

and by the time you know it—

it's been a lifetime.

That's how it works.

You never quite find love.
It finds you

and reveals itself
when you least expect it to.

All the time.

NEEDED MOST

That's expected of you.

To look for help,

for someone to pour yourself to
when you need it most.

Because no one
wants to deal

with heart shattering things
on their own.

Human beings are social creatures

and everyone needs someone
to feel them.

To sit down and talk.
To share a cup of coffee with

and explore themselves.

So ask for help.

Seek it.

I advise you to.

Complete solitude should never
be an option
because you have plenty

of people
who genuinely care.

People who feel
the same way,

who are currently going
through moments

just as bad as you are.

All you have to do
is overcome the fear

of being judged
and overcome yourself

for what you feel.

Everything else
will always fall

into place.

Just remember

to give yourself

to people with an open heart.

To say what's on your mind
and to never isolate yourself

from people
when you *need* them most.

SELF-LOVE

Self-love is about survival.

About finding your own
path and passing through.

It's not about
the opinions of others.

It's not about
holding on to the things
that bring you harm—

to the things
that hurt.

It's not about
forgetting who you are—

what you want
and need.

No, never that.

In detail,
it's about you.

About watering your own soul
the best way

you know how.

It's about finding
your own truth—

about knowing
what kind of love
you deserve.

And it's something
that can't be taught
but earned.

It's something
that's not given freely

but obtained through experience
and struggle.

And it's not easy.

It's one of the hardest things
to do, let alone practice.

But once you know it.

Once you finally accept yourself
for who you are,

then,
it becomes

somewhat of a miracle.

It becomes a blessing,
and it is one

only you can give
to yourself.

So this I tell you,

in all truth and rawness.

Life is too short
not to love yourself

and in some sense,
you deserve to find
your perfect happiness,

no matter what kind
of lies

you've been told.

THE SHORELINE

Sometimes,

you feel like you've spent
your whole life

planning

for a future that isn't certain.

Chasing a love
that doesn't exist.

And worrying about
a past that doesn't even matter.

And this is what your life
has turned into.

Stressing over the unknown.
Overthinking about people
you've never even met

and dwelling in moments
that drown you,

instead of the ones
that push you
toward the shore.

DO NOT TAKE

Don't take yourself
too seriously.

Don't spend your days
working too hard

and don't spend your nights
overthinking
the future.

Don't mistreat people
and don't pretend

to be

something you're not.

Don't judge others
based on your own life

and don't hold on
when there's nothing left

to hold on to.

Don't wait
if you're not expecting
and don't think you know

when you really don't.

Don't laugh
if you don't want to

and don't take people
for granted.

So many don'ts
in this list, some obvious too.

But the problem is,

you know what's wrong
and still,

there will be times
you will ignore it.

And you will follow
your heart

even if it means harm.

That's human life.

We experience tragedies
and sometimes it's our own fault.

And sometimes
we can't control

the outcome—

sometimes

we'll do what's wrong
because we'll feel

as if

it's the right thing
to do.

The fire burns,
and our hands have scars,

and we'll lean over
because we want to.

Every, single, time.

NANCY

Nancy, a young brunette,

a friend of mine for many years.

She only calls me
when she needs me.

When she feels alone.

Most of the time
she rants about the man
she is currently seeing.

She says how much
he doesn't appreciate her.

How much
he takes everything she does
for him for granted.

Of course
there is another side
to the story.

And if you've ever been
on the side
that gives the advice,
you know how people

never tend to say
their faults in the situation.

They just pick at the person
they're complaining about

and ignore
the cause to their troubles.

Nancy,
being Nancy,

a smart, witty girl
with a little darkness

and what she doesn't say is…

how she pushes people away.

She has this terrible
little temper.

This little tick, a silent rage.

She looks into everything.
She is paranoid and believes

everyone she is with
is bound to be her doom.

In other words,

she doesn't trust anyone.

No matter how long
she's been with them.

It's always the same story.

"No one cares,"
she says, over the phone.

"Everyone is all the same."

My dear,
when will you learn?

That it is not that you can't
trust anyone.

It is more
that you cannot trust
yourself.

She doesn't let people in
unless it's her way

and then she wonders
why no one ever takes

the time
to try and save her.
Why no one ever seems

to care enough.

Or love her
the way she needs
to be loved.

And it is easy to point out.

That she is
how she is

because she has not
only failed to understand,

but also

has failed
to love herself.

A LONG LIST

I have a long list
of people I've done wrong,

of people
I've tried to love
but have failed.

And I'm not proud of it.

I don't take credit
for breaking people's hearts.

For falling in love with them—
to suddenly leave them behind.

The thing is,

and maybe I'm the only person
who feels this way,

but I don't know
who I am at times.

I don't know
what to feel—what to say
or think.

I could wake up one day

and be totally in love with something,

with you

and then the next day
wake up

wanting to be left alone—isolated,

somewhere in some place
that has yet to be discovered.

This is the way
my heart works

and I've learned this.

I'm trying to adapt
to the way I change.

Because some nights,
I feel like I'm on top of the world

while other nights
I feel like I'm buried beneath it.

And this is what
depression feels like.

Like I'm two different people
and both of them

barely know who they are.

They sit alone in table
and they barely

understand themselves.

IMPORTANT CHOICES

There comes a time
when you must make
a choice.

And I don't mean,
one of those silly little choices

between what shoes to wear
or pants to put on.

I mean
the kind of choice

that is going to change
your life forever.

Because bad things are going to happen
and some good things, too

but it's how you let them
affect you.

That within itself
is the most important choice
of them all.

SWEET GIRL

My sweet girl,
I see you now running across
the living room.

Laughing without a clue
of how hard this life is going
to be to you.

It almost hurts me.

The fact that at this moment
you believe your world

is perfect
and it is,

that is, for what it is.

You're still a little girl.

You have so much
to grow into.

So much room to fill.
So much pain to go through.

So much suffering
you'll never expect

to happen.

My sweet girl.
My sweet little girl.

In all your glory
you're running across
without a care.

If there is anything I can do,

anything you can remember
whenever you feel the aches

of your heart or
the tears flowing from your eyes

or the intensity
you will carry within your
bones.

If there is anything
I can do,

it is to tell you
that all things pass.

That all pain eventually
dissolves.

That time heals everything

and what it doesn't

you have to step away
and learn to heal
on your own.

My sweet girl.

With every fiber in your body,
every atom,
and every connection...

know,

that yes,
life is hard.

Losing people is hard.
Losing opportunities is hard.

Losing love is hard.

But losing yourself
in what hurts
is even harder.

Just believe
that somewhere within you

there is a special kind
of light.

It is the kind
that can overcome

any kind
of darkness.

All you have to do
is close your eyes
and remember…

what it was like
when you were just
a little girl

because
that will always

represent
the best parts of me

and also

the best parts
of you.

TIME LOSS

The first half
of your life

you'll spend
acquiring wealth

and social status.

And the second half
of your life,

you'll spend learning
how the first half

of your life
really meant nothing
at all.

THE NEXT TIME

Do not become
one of those people

who become dependent
on the person you love.

You know,
that kind of person

that once they feel
as if they've found someone

they ignore
everyone who's been there
for them.

Do not become this person.

Do not forget the people
you have around you.

Do not ignore them
because for the time being

you feel as if
you have the one
you need.

Do not become this type of person.

No one wants to be
this person

but almost too often
do they become it.

So please,
for Christ's sake,

the next time you find yourself
in a hot pile of love,

do not detach yourself
from your friends.

From your family.
From the people who really care.

Because lovers come and go.

Some hurt you
and some heal you

but those who've watched you grow
are something else.

It is something
you can't put into words.

It is something you just feel,
you know?

So please,
do not become this person.

You owe it to the people
who care

to be so much more
than that.

I hope you take this with you.

Now good-bye.

MISS YOU MISS THEM

People will miss you
the moment you stop caring.

The moment you moved on.
Because that's how it works.

Most people only want
what no longer belongs to them,

what they once had
but failed to appreciate.

And it's sad,
you know?

Because you can spend
so much time devoted

to someone
while feeling ignored,

but the moment you realize
your worth,
things begin to change.

You begin to do things
for yourself.

You begin to see the light,
feel it and become it.

You move on to bigger
and better things.

You meet different people
and for a moment

you find yourself being happy.

And it's just sad
but also very good

because you had to let go
of someone who was once

important to you
to find yourself again.

You had to water your own soul
and find your own smile.

And you spent
and wasted so much time
doing so,

without knowing
how to love yourself before.

And that's what's terrible here.

That's the tragedy.

How you always need someone
to help you discover your worth

and how you always need
to lose someone you once cared about.

Need someone
you once loved

to dig a hole in you,
in order for you to finally

learn to appreciate yourself
for who you are.

FIGHT WARS

We fight their wars.

We come home
and they give us a statue.

We die for what they believe in.

We come home
and they give us a metal.

They praise us for our bravery…
for how we fought each night.

And then,
we come back home.

They take away our businesses.
They take away our culture.
They take away our pride and legacy.

And then,
they wonder why none of us
truly succeed.

Not unless we work for them.
Not unless we join their revolution.

One built on blood,

sweat, tears and sacrifice.

We fight their wars,
my love,
my people

because if we do not
we are thrown
to the wolves,

in jail to rot.

And then,
some of us don't even make it
back home.

No,
instead,

we come back
in a box full of metals

and maybe,
if we were lucky,

we get a statue
with our name.

I COULD ALMOST

I could almost feel
my heart beating.

I am not dead yet.

There's still a fight in me—
a will I cannot describe.

If anything I have done
has been meaningful

throughout the years,
writing has got to be it.

The dark room
swallows the walls.

The bed headboard
and the ceilings.

Writing.

It has got to be
all for the art.

For the words
that I do not know enough.

The plasma screen blinks.

Bright,
out the window

the street lamp flickers.

All is calm, quiet.

All except
what lies beneath my chest,
behind my eyes.

I could now feel it,
my heart.

Alive and well.

Strong yet weak
and fragile.

Welcoming to all things
that shatter.

Relating to it.

Picking out the similarities
and saying, you're like me.

You're not alone.

Although,
we are not the same.

I lie here.

Listening to the air conditioner.
Listening to the loud sounds
that dwell deep within my ears.

The OM.

The humming of life
and death.

The never-ending beep,
that only surfaces when no one
is around.

I write more.

These words.

As if I feel
even more confused
than ever.

As the paranoia kicks in.

I am not alone.

No one understands.

They never do,
although they want to.

Perhaps, it is me,
and I am not clear enough.

But none of that matters.

Nothing ever does
unless it affects your life.

I mean,
it really has to change it.

Other than that,
it is all a shot in the dark.

You know,
a shot within a shot.

Who knows.

But I'm still here…

for reasons unknown
but the words…

my incoherent thoughts.

The loss of one's mind.

I am forgetting
and it all feels like a dream.

All things,
most things,

gone

like a year-old love letter.

Ignored and uncared for.

This is me.

My words are me
and it either makes sense to you
or not.

But like I said,
none of it matters.

It only does
if it means something

and if it changes your life
for good.

LAUGH IT OFF

Now imagine that,
all the bridges I had to burn.

All the people
I had to leave behind.

All the times
I had to say good-bye…

the times I had
to reinvent myself

and the times
I had to tell myself
to keep going.

Now imagine this,

all the bridges
I had to rebuild.

All the people
I had to chase.

All the times
I said hello…

the times

I broke down
and the times

I found more.

I hope one day,
we find each other again
and laugh

over whatever pain
we might have caused.

NOTHING MORE OR LESS

When it's time for you
to love,

you're going to love.

The same way
when it's time for you to hurt,

you're going to hurt.

Your life
is perfectly balanced.

You will hurt
and love
when it is necessary.

Nothing more.
Nothing less.

MOODS

I go through moods
when I love people

and then
I go through moments

when I wish
I was the last person
alive,

when I wish
I was a legend.

And this is one
of those times,
the bad times.

When I was in high school,
I wasn't outspoken.

I wasn't the popular guy,
in fact,

for reasons unknown
I managed to be barely

noticeable.

I always kept low
and only kept a few

good comrades
around me.

We did graffiti.
We made music.
We drank beers.
We fought.

We got in trouble
with the cops.

Hell,
we even went
to jail a few times.

The chaos of my adolescence.

After all of that,
still,
nobody cared.

Growing up
nobody cared,

not unless you had
something they wanted
and most of the time

it was about image,
about being cool,
looking cool.

You know,
things that have
no true force.

Things that are illusions.
Things that do no matter.

It was only then,
when I began college

that people began
to notice me

for my art,
for my ability
to sculpt and paint.

They came in herds
asking for help
and I gave it

everytime.

Soon after,
when I graduated
no one seemed to come around.

Not until
I began to work

at Univision
as an art director.

That's when
they came for me again,
for help,

for anything
I could do
to get them a gig
in the network.

When I left Univision,
soon after,

they disappeared again
and it wasn't until

my writing situation
took off on social media

when the oceans of people
returned.

They returned for something,
for help,
for a piece of what I built.

Whether it was
help building their brand,
money or fame.

They never stopped
coming for more.

People I hadn't spoken to
in years appeared,
and people I didn't even know

out of the blue
wanted to *"help me"*

and everything for *"me."*
But in the end,

it was always for
their own personal gain.

I got smarter.
I got colder.

And now
I understand why
some of the most successful people

suffer from depression
and why they feel
most alone.

It's a never-ending love song.

People will always be looking
for an easy way out
and they will use you,

take everything from you
while you're not looking

and forget you
the moment they take
what you have.

Their interest,
like a thirst,

and once they start
it's very hard
to run away from.

They are wolves
in sheep's clothing

but I have always been
a lion trapped

in an unlocked cage.

AMEN.

I WONDER ABOUT YOU

You can break
all of me

but for
Christ's sake

do not touch
my hands.

Let them be,
for I need them

to hold you
through the night.

I need them
to keep you company

whenever you
feel

like running away
from it all.

NOTICE YOU

I have this feeling
that you want me

to believe
that you're broken,

that you're this miserable
lonely person.

This human being
that endures

all types of hurting,
right?

But I think you're wrong.
I know deep down

within you,
within that hurting body
there's more

and it's something
beyond what the eye could see.

And I know
it's ferocious.

It doesn't contain fear.

You're strong
but that doesn't mean
you have to be alone.

People love you,
so you should *let them*
love you.

People will always notice you
for who you really are.

SMART, STRONG AND INTELLIGENT

I knew I loved her
because she loved life.

She cared for it
as if any moment

she might slip away.

To where?

That's something
I'll never know

but it's not like
it mattered…

for whether she stayed
or left me behind,

I'd still love her.

I'd still need her,
want her

and it would be
same way

any other man
would want his woman.

Smart,
strong
and intelligent.

Never weak
and too beautiful
to ignore.

SUPPOSED TO BE

Of course,
you feel like
you can't trust her,

I mean,
a woman like that
is surreal,
like a dream.

with fierce eyes
as if she were made up

in the minds
of a hundred mad men.

She's *too much*
to handle,

too much woman
for the average man,

by that, I mean,

one minute
she's the center of a storm,
calm and collected

and then,

the next second,
she's walking on the edge
of chaos,

the sun
and where all things go

to dissolve into
thin air.

You inhale,
grasp for what is not there.

And sure,
she makes you feel

uncomfortable.

She's supposed to
do that.

She's supposed to
make you feel as if

you're not sure
about anything,

not this world
or the next.

Not life or death.

Not love or loneliness.

And now
since there is
nothing for you,

nothing to rely on…
you leave,

walk out on the things
that scare you.

Things that put
the fear of the unknown
before you…

but,

before you go
and release her
into the wild,

where she came from,
where she might forget
who you are.

Always remember

how the two of you
are not the same.

How you may think
you understand her,

know her
and feel her

because you've spent
a few nights with her...

but you're not.

In fact,
you know nothing
of her
as many men do.

And remember this,
she's a wild card

and just because
you can't handle her

doesn't mean
she wants you to
in the first place.

She's more,
more than you could
break down.

She's the core

of what moves,

the heat that slowly
converts all the people

she loves
into clouds.

She's the maker
of dreams,

the inspiration
that's needed to change

the dark to light.

She's the complex
drift of the moon

and the gentle pull
of the tide.

Goddammit
men like you
fear perfection.

And that's why
you don't understand her
and it's okay
if you don't,

but please,
for the love you haven't
tasted,

don't destroy her.

For she's a flower,
so if you want nothing

with her,
then by all means,

let her bloom,
let her roam

freely

and let her be.

LET IT

You can't stop love.

You can't beat it either
but *it can* beat the oxygen
out of your body.

And it is strong enough
to kill you,
to destroy an entire building
without the use of bombs.

You can't stop love,
that is never
going to happen,
the same way you can't stop
death or birth

or laughter
or pain
or all the things
that rush toward your life

for better or worse.

You can't stop love,
so let it happen.

Let it give you all the stupid

little reasons to do it,
to find it.

You can't stop love.
Youcan't stop anything
from happening...

so let it.

Let it.
Let it...

all consume
you.

REGRETS

Sometimes
it feel like I am moving
backward

and sometimes
the past is all I have
to remind me

that I should have
loved you

a little harder.

A TRIP THROUGH THE DAY

When I saw
the love of my life
pass by.

It was the first
day of class
and I was in my third
semester in college.

I was taking
a time base media course
and I was waiting outside
of the classroom,

that is,
waiting for the professor
to arrive.

While I was waiting,
I saw my breath flow
out of me
to mock me
and tease me
of my own words.

Then a goddess
with long swaying hair,
big sad eyes

and mouthful of glitter
as if she had tasted
the night sky…

caught my attention
from a far.

Of course
my heart was on my sleeve.
My eyes were looking
at the dirt
and my soul
far off to some distant place.

We spoke briefly.
She was looking for her class.

Soon enough she had to go
and she went off
into the buildings

into the backdrop
like a wild fox
running out of a
burning forest.

That was five years ago.

Now
instead of remembering
her skin,

her eyes,
her lips and hair,

all I could remember
was what I last
said to her
the very last moment
we shared.

"I hope I see you around."

I never saw her again,
although
I wish I had.

It was just,
that,
something inside of me
wished I had said
something better,
something worthwhile,

something that would make her
remember me.

Now the reason,
I'm here,
writing this down

is this....
about a month ago,

I ran into her
and once again,
she was gone.

I watched her pass by me
without exchanging
a single word.

And to think,
there goes
the love of my life,
perhaps.

A woman
I could have loved.

A woman
I could have
grown old with.

A woman
who could have known
all of my secrets.

But in the end,
she's just another woman
I never had
the courage to meet.

Another *"what if"*
lost in the thread of time.

ALL IS GOOD

The only thing
wrong with our love

is the
way we exceed
to love others

but barely had enough

to love
ourselves.